For my Friends and Family

The Anchor Still Holds

Facing the Unknown

Colette Atkinson

APOSOTLIC PUBLISHING CO
SINCE 2016

The Anchor Still Holds: Facing the Unknown by Colette Atkinson

Published by Apostolic Publishing Company
Lumberton, Ms 39455
www.apostolicpublishing.co

Editor: Sonja Baker

All scriptures are from the KJV Bible unless otherwise noted.

Scripture quotations from The Authorized (King James) Version. Rights in the
Authorized Version in the United Kingdom are vested in the Crown. Reproduced by
permission of the Crown's patentee, Cambridge University Press

Scripture quotations marked (NLT) are taken from the Holy Bible, New Living
Translation, copyright © 1996, 2004, 2007 by Tyndale House Foundation. Used by
permission of Tyndale House Publishers, Inc., Carol Stream, IL 60188. All rights
reserved.

ISBN: 978-0-9976313-8-8
Printed in USA

Acknowledgments

My deepest desire is to win souls for His kingdom. I want to start by honoring my Heavenly Father, the Lord Jesus Christ, who was, who is, and is to come. The great I Am, forever He reigns in Heaven and earth. He has granted me the privilege of writing this book.

Thank you to everyone who encouraged me to press on while writing. To my close family and friends who have lifted me in prayer and carried me through the difficult times of my life. To my Triumphant family, how could I ever forget those precious, yet trying moments you prayed for my family. Many more people I can say, and you know who you are. May God's blessings be with you all.

To my mother, Jennifer Ivoree Atkinson, also known as "Moy," the wind beneath my wings. Thank you for giving birth to me and helping guide me to be the woman I am today. You have shown me the importance of placing God first in all things. You taught me how important it is to be a servant of God…selfless, kind, and loving.

To my loving father, Keith Atkinson, who spoke the Living Word in our ears from childhood. Thank you for molding me into the woman I am today. I love you, Dad!

To my kind-hearted sister, Kristina Atkinson, whom I thank God for always. You are stronger than you think, with great purpose. You took over Mom's kitchen with compassion to serve God by serving others, through feeding family, friends, and even strangers you've never met. I give much appreciation to you for all that you do and for always having my back!

To my niece, Demoya Ivoree Reid, and nephew, Daniel Emmanuel Atkinson Smith, I feel like I gave birth to the two of you. I pray earnestly for you daily that God's perfect will be done in your life. Aunty Colette "Allie" loves you both!

Thank you to my destiny helpers, divinely sent by the Lord: Minister Campbell, Mama Rose Atkinson, Cadia Chambers, and Simone McDonald-Walker. My life wouldn't be the same without you.

Introduction

As you read this book, I pray that God will speak to you in a personal way. The Holy Spirit, as promised to each of us after Jesus Christ died and rose from the grave, is our teacher to guide us into all truth. Throughout these pages you will find the the truth of God's Word, testimonies of His faithfulness, and a glimpse of a life that was well lived by my dearest mother:

Jennifer Ivoree Atkinson

I'll forever love you mom.
- Colette

Contents

Facing the Unknown   1

Faith Without Borders   9

Praising Through the Storm   19

Selfless Love   25

Answering the Call   31

The Grace of God   37

There is a Lamb   43

I Am the Way   49

Are You Saved?   57

I Saw the Lord   69

A Collection of Testimonies   77

Chapter 1

Facing the Unknown

"Be careful for nothing; but in everything by prayer and supplication with thanksgiving let your request be made known unto God. And the peace of God, which passeth all understanding, shall keep your hearts and minds through Christ Jesus" – Philippians 4:6–7

What is life? Many ask this question when faced with trials, tribulations, or circumstances. Every day, we are faced with unknowns. For no one knows what tomorrow will bring but God.

His Word declares in Isaiah 55: 8-9, *"For my thoughts are not your thoughts, neither are your ways my ways, saith the Lord, for as the heavens are higher than the earth, so are my ways higher than your ways, and my thoughts than your thoughts."* Clearly, we see in this verse that we humans can never fathom God's mind. His thoughts are far greater than we can ever imagine.

The Word also declares in Job 11:7, *"Canst thou by searching find out God? Canst thou find out the Almighty into perfection?"* If we search the scriptures, we can find many examples that reveal God's plan through different people. Everything they faced worked out for the Glory of God without knowing in advance what the outcome would be.

The story of Joseph is a perfect example! In the book of Genesis, a young man named Joseph was sold into slavery by his brothers and many others, but God used this evil act to place Joseph in a position of power, which God then used to save his brothers (Genesis 50:20).

Humans face the unknown daily, for we do not know what the next moment will bring. When we wake up in the morning, despite our plans, we cannot see what lies ahead. Therefore, we must always place God first in all things so we can be spiritually vigilant about His plans.

How do we take the first step in doing this? Faith! The Bible declares in Hebrew 11:6, *"But without faith it is impossible to please Him: for He that cometh to God must believe that He is and that He is a rewarder of them that diligently seek Him.*" God wants to take us to a place of faith without borders. In doing so, we must first believe who He says He is. John 3:16 reads, *"For God so loved the world that He gave His only begotten son that whosoever believeth in Him shall not perish but have everlasting life."*

To walk in the will of God, we have to believe and have faith. This is the only way to overcome the obstacles we will face in life. God sent His Son, Jesus Christ, so that we might have life and life more abundantly...not only on this earth but also in Heaven.

It all started on May 21st. Mom wasn't feeling well, but despite her pain, she persevered and continued to serve others in need, care for her family, and go to work. She always would say, "I have to go to work; they need me. Dr. Elmousely has a case today, and I can't call out." The look on our faces would prompt her to continue, "It's ok, Mom will be all right. I'll get rest when I get home".

She loved her job. It was her family away from home. She had such zeal to help others relentlessly in whatever way she could. Selfless is the best word to describe her. She never took a moment to stop and think about herself first but always considered others.

Mom finally decided she couldn't push against this pain anymore. Driving herself to the hospital ended up leading to her being admitted for further evaluation. And, then more than five days of an unknown mystery. My heart was beating, my mind racing, wondering what could be causing the pain that became too much for Mom to bear.

My mother, also known as 'Moy,' her pet name given by a child in Jamaica, was strong. Nothing stopped her from doing what she was determined to do. But this pain was more than she could handle. Thankfully, pain medication and IV fluids helped to relieve the discomfort she felt throughout the days after her hospital admission.

The first night in the hospital, the doctors thought her gall bladder needed to be removed. I felt relief that night, thinking she would probably be home soon once they did the surgery to remove it. She encouraged me to go to work for the night and said she would be fine.

After leaving work the next morning, I had a mandatory class to attend. Anxious and overwhelmed,

I couldn't wait to leave. I rushed back to the hospital with the expectation that everything was going smoothly, but that wasn't the case. One of the doctors, Dr. Zoha, who Mom had worked with for many years, said to her, "Jennifer, we can't operate to remove your gall bladder because there is more that we need to look at." Certain blood levels were rising, which caused Dr. Zoha to suspect this was more serious.

With multiple scans over the five days of her admission, they finally could see something that might be causing the pain, but it was hard to detect. Eventually, they discovered a small shadow of something on her pancreas close to the portal vein. A tumor was the culprit. As it was located in a delicate and vascular area in her body, the doctors had to take precautions to do a biopsy. They needed to identify whether or not it was cancerous. Facing the unknown, my sister, dad, I, and many others were praying, fasting, and seeking God, hoping it was not cancer.

Dr. Zoha booked Mom the following day for a specialist to perform the biopsy. My grandmother and I sat in the waiting area...along with Sister Rose, a very close family friend. We were all anxious to see Mom come through this procedure.

Hours later, the doctor approached us to say she could not get a good tumor sample due to the high risk of bleeding. I didn't want it to be seen, but I was falling apart within my heart, crying out to the good Lord to help us be strong. Exercising patience during this time was difficult, but God saw us through it each day.

A week before Mom went into the hospital, I dreamed I was at my parents' house, entertaining visitors and eating. A messenger (I couldn't see their face) approached me to say a storm was coming and to prepare everyone for what was to come. The Lord, so full of grace and mercy, used a dream to caution and reassure me that He would be with us through it all. This dream gave me comfort in facing the unknown each day. Although my flesh wanted to fall apart, the Almighty God strengthened my inner spirit.

As we walked to Mom's room, waiting for the nurse to send her back, I ran into my Mom's friend Ann, a Physician Assistant. She is one of the most beautiful souls I've ever met. She held me in her arms, tears streaming down her face. With great hesitation, she told me, "The doctors think it's pancreatic cancer, but they needed the biopsy to confirm it." I held her tight and said it would be okay; God is in control. I realized at that moment that it was not only our family that was hurting, but it was her coworkers and many others who loved her dearly and felt our pain in these trying moments.

How does one function when facing the unknown? The key word is "prayer!" At the beginning of this chapter, the scripture Philippians 4:6 states, *"Be careful for nothing; but in everything by prayer and supplication with thanksgiving let your requests be made known unto God."* I want to take the time to highlight the next verse, 7, which states, *"And the peace of God, which passeth all understanding, shall keep your hearts and minds through Christ Jesus."*

According to the NLT version of the Bible, Paul was imploring the Philippian Church not to worry about anything but to pray about everything. We must tell God what we need and thank Him for all He has done. Then, once we do that, we will experience God's peace, which exceeds anything we can understand.

Despite the storm we were facing, the peace of God was guarding our hearts as a family in this difficult time. I often felt as if my world was turned upside down, but living in Christ Jesus each day sprang forth a well of living water within my soul that kept me.

Have you ever experienced the peace of God? If you haven't yet, all you have to do is come to Him. John 14:27 declares, *"Peace I leave with you, my peace I give unto you: not as the world giveth, give I unto you. Let not your heart be troubled, neither let it be afraid."* Christ came for all that we might have life and experience God's peace in this world full of darkness.

Chapter 2

Faith Without Borders

"Therefore we are always confident, knowing that, whilst we are at home in the body, we are absent from the Lord: (For we walk by faith, not by sight :) We are confident, I say, and willing rather to be absent from the body, and to be present with Lord" – 2 Corinthians 5:6-8

As we read the above scripture verses, we find that the writer of Corinthians, Paul the Apostle, speaks of the importance of being confident in the Lord. Our faith gives us victory to overcome the world, as it is written in 1 John 5:4: *"For every child of God defeats this evil world, and we achieve this victory through our faith"* (NLT). It is easy to tell someone to walk by faith and not by sight when, as humans, we naturally tend to walk with our eyes open, wanting to believe what we see. But truth be known, we find what we do not see impossible to believe.

The Bible declares in Hebrews 11:1, *"Now faith is the substance of things hoped for, the evidence of things not seen."* As humans, our Heavenly Father knows that we can only walk by faith with His power and His strength. Although the first step is to allow Jesus Christ into our hearts, believing that He is the Son of the living God who came to die for us so that we can be reconciled back to our Father in Heaven. There is so much more than that.

Faith without borders is where God wants to take us as believers in Christ, having a personal relationship with God and taking our faith to a place without borders. It's a place where our human flesh must die! A place where the impossibilities become possibilities! A place that takes you beyond what our finite minds can ever fathom.

The Bible states in Romans 11:34, *"For who hath known the mind of the Lord? Or who hath been his counsellor?"* Another scripture that the Holy Spirit leads me to as I'm writing is 1 Corinthians 3:19-20, *"For the wisdom of this world is foolishness with God. For it is written, He taketh the wise in their own craftiness. And again, the Lord knoweth the thoughts of the wise, that they are vain"*.

Mom, Dad, and I took the drive to Albany, New York,

to see a different doctor who was more experienced in obtaining the biopsy. The nurse who prepared her for the procedure was very kind to Mom. So much so that Mom gave her the Victoria's Secret bag in which she carried her belongings. Joyfully, she used a hospital bag instead to place her personal items. She enjoyed giving to others, even if it was to someone she did not know.

Dad and I sat together in the family room, waiting for the doctor to come out and speak with us. As it was previously, my insides were filled with nervousness and anxiety filled the room. Waiting to hear the results of Mom's biopsy was not easy. To pass the time, I was reading a book by Kathryn Kuhlman called *I Believe in Miracles*. My faith stirred up within me that day as I read the miracles God manifested through Kathryn.

Deep within, I was praying and saying Lord, whatever is there, remove it, and if it is possible, let the doctors not find anything. With all my heart, I believed that whatever the results were, I was confident that God could heal. It's the worst place to be, waiting to hear the news, not knowing whether it will be good or bad.

After a while, the doctor finally came out. He brought Dad and me into the family meeting room and explained that he was able to get the biopsy but didn't like how the tumor looked. He told us there was a strong chance it was cancerous, but we would have to wait for the results. He would call us as soon as it was made available to him.

Amidst all the waiting, the most remarkable thing was the peace of God that anchored our hearts. Yes, we all were concerned and battled with fear, but confidence in Christ made the difference.

The days passed by slowly as we anticipated hearing from the doctor.

On June 4th, in the early afternoon, Mom answered the phone. As she said, "Yes, this is Jennifer Atkinson." All our eyes turned in her direction, waiting and hoping it was not what they suspected. As I saw her facial expression change and the tears that started streaming down her face, I knew it wasn't good. Even though deep within, I hoped to hear that the biopsy was negative…I knew.

As Mom hung up the phone, she said, "It's cancer. Pancreatic cancer." We all stared at each other silently as we sat in the living room. "Where did this come from?" Mom said with a soft voice. Worried in our hearts, we began to cry. But it didn't take long before we stopped, held hands, and prayed.

Dad immediately said, "Hunny, I know this is not what we wanted to hear, but God is with you; He will see us through this, and His will shall be done."

We all sat together, trying to digest this news. The only thing we knew we could do to comfort Mom in this moment was to continue in prayer. Prayer is the key! There is nothing else to do in times like these but cry out to the Lord in prayer. In this particular moment, we only had our faith to hold onto and trust that God would take us through this storm.

Mom started making phone calls to share the news. It wasn't easy trying to figure out where to begin.

According to research and statistics, pancreatic cancer is one of the most aggressive cancers. However, my faith in God started to rise and go beyond borders like never before.

When we began to seek physicians, and they would explain how serious this was, deep within, my faith would allow me to open my mouth to declare to the doctors,

"But GOD!" No matter what came in our storm, I didn't back down from the promises of God. My mind would reflect on the many miraculous stories I've read in the Bible that caused me to believe. And if God said greater works than these we shall do in His name, He could do the same for Mom.

The beautiful Word of God declares in John 14:12, *"Verily, verily, I say unto you, He that believeth on me, the works that I do shall he do also; and greater works than these shall he do; because I go unto my Father."* The scripture further states in verse 14, *"If ye shall ask anything in my name, I will do it."*

As the Holy Spirit reminded me of His promising Word, my faith continued to be lifted to a place it had never been before, despite the fear that crept in to try and take away my hope that Jesus has the power to heal Mom. I even told myself how ironic it was that I started to read a book called *I Believe in Miracles*. This boosted my faith that truly nothing is impossible with my God!

It was June 19th and Mom had her first appointment to start her chemotherapy. We were not excited or pleased about it; however, at this point, we didn't want to wait too long to start treatment. We heard how aggressive this cancer can be and that people usually do not survive long after being diagnosed.

It was at this point in our lives that the struggle began. We didn't have time to sit down and breathe. But, we had to think fast about how to treat this monster named cancer.

Sitting beside Mom, I watched the nurse start the chemo through the IV. It broke my heart. But with the strength of God, I held onto her hands tightly to reassure her that she would never be alone on this journey.

As the weeks turned into months, we witnessed her losing weight, unable to keep down food at times due to the side effects from the chemo and the disease that had invaded her body. Many times, as I watched her eat, I prayed that the food would stay down.

Mom, known for being one of the strongest women we knew, endured much pain and suffering, but she never gave up. She continued to believe and have faith. If the God she served, who had brought her this far in her life, did it before, He would do it again.

I can clearly remember her sitting up in bed, sewing

her pillows with a smile as if it were yesterday. She said, "Colette, you don't worry. Mommy is going to be okay; it is well with my soul. Whatever God's will is for my life, *it is well.*"

She told me stories of being a young girl growing up on the Island of Jamaica and how God always answered her prayers. One such prayer was for God to send her a husband without children and that he would love the Lord. God answered and gave her the desire of her heart.

Growing up as a child, she saw men abuse other women. She was raised by her grandmother, who fulfilled both roles of mother and father. As she spoke about many testimonies from the Lord, she had a peace that no matter what the outcome, she would still say, "*It is well.*" On that day, hearing her say these words in her room gave me inner peace because she truly exemplified faith without borders!

Abraham was called a friend of God, not because God loved him any greater, but because of his faith. It states in James 2:23, *"And the scripture was fulfilled which saith, Abraham believed God, and it was imputed unto him for righteousness: and he was called the friend of God."* Being a friend of God is possible if we believe in and trust Him. There is a song that says, *"Through it all, I have learned to trust in Jesus; I've learned to trust in God."* Through all our trials, tribulations, and circumstances, God teaches us to trust in Him. This is our faith without borders.

Growing up, I was always afraid to learn how to swim. Despite my fear, I loved the sea water but always stayed in the shallow end because I feared drowning. God used this as an illustration to reveal that He wants our faith to become like an object floating in the sea. Even though you know the waters are deep, don't be afraid, for we are being carried in the arms of Jesus.

One of the known apostles in the Bible, Peter, walked out of a boat towards Jesus when Jesus said for him to come. But as he walked out on the water and saw the wind, he became afraid and began to sink, crying out for the Lord to save him. Once Jesus reached out and caught him by his hand, He said to Peter, *"You of little faith, why did you doubt Me?"* (Matt 14:22-23).

Have you been praying for your faith to go beyond borders? Do you believe it is possible? Jesus gives everyone faith. Do you use it? It will be given if we open our hearts to receive by believing. It's never too late; for as long as there is life, there is hope.

In the midst of "Facing the Unknown," I challenge you to go into the deep, trusting in Jesus will take you there. I guarantee you that you will experience His everlasting peace.

Chapter 3

Praising Through the Storm

*"To appoint unto them that mourn in Zion,
to give unto them beauty for ashes, the oil of
joy for mourning, the garment of praise for
the spirit of heaviness; that they might be
called trees of righteousness, the planting of
the Lord, that he might be glorified"*
— Isaiah 61:3

At least once in our lifetime, we will face storms that trouble our minds. As we encounter these storms, heaviness comes upon us, causing fear and worry to cripple our faith. How do you tell someone or yourself to praise God during the storm? We may say it, but experiencing it is different. Isaiah 61:3 speaks loudly about the good news for the oppressed: God will give us the garment of praise in exchange for the Spirit of heaviness.

Throughout history, ashes have represented loss and

mourning. But here, I believe Isaiah wanted the reader to arise amid our heaviness and praise the Lord. Now, telling a non-believer this wouldn't make much sense to them. However, if you have a personal relationship with the Lord Jesus Christ, God's Word will be your guide and help you embrace it. The Lord Jesus Christ has already paid the price in full on the cross of Calvary…and His sacrifice provides beauty for ashes.

A precious oil of joy comes from our Savior in our times of mourning. When we put on the garment of praise for the Spirit of heaviness, the burdens will roll off our shoulders. How do we get to this place? Psalms 1:2-3 declares, *"But his delight is in the law of the Lord; and in his law doth he meditate day and night. And he shall be like a tree planted by the rivers of water, that bringeth forth his fruit in his season; his leaf also shall not wither; and whatsoever he doeth shall prosper"*. Jesus is the Living Word, and we must delight in that Word day and night to experience His peace. He will keep us rooted and grounded when facing the unknown.

As you pray, ask the Lord to give you the desire to delight in the Lord and place a hunger in your soul to meditate upon His Holy Word. If we ask anything in His name, He will do it, according to His Word

(John 14:14), for God is not a man that He should lie (Numbers 23:19). Try Him for yourself, and you shall see!

Continuing the journey with Mom as she began her chemotherapy was one of the most painful things to bear. I could only sit and watch as the nurse infused this seemingly deadly chemical through her veins. Of course, before consenting to the treatment, you hear all the possible side effects. And then there is a chance that it may not be effective.

According to [1]ScienceDirect, a study completed in the year 2020 reports, "Pancreatic adenocarcinoma (PAC) is the seventh leading cause of cancer-related death in both sexes, causing more than 331,000 deaths per year globally. An estimation of 174,650 new cases was expected to be diagnosed in the USA with 45,750 deaths expected to occur in 2019."

About a month before her admission to the hospital, one of the first symptoms Mom experienced was back pain and sharp abdominal pain. Her pain was not consistent, albeit unbearable, so much so that she couldn't wait any longer to find out the cause.

We traveled from Poughkeepsie to New York City to one of the most well-known research hospitals, Sloan Kettering. The doctor looked at Mom and said he had never seen anyone come to him with newly diagnosed pancreatic cancer at an early stage. He said Mom was at stage 2 or 3, with no surgical intervention recommended. This was due to the increased risk of fatal bleeding because of the location of the tumor.

Since we would have to travel back and forth from Poughkeepsie to NYC, we decided to stay in Poughkeepsie for treatment. Thankfully, they offered the same treatment that the doctor at Sloan Kettering advised.

Mom was a trooper, a fighter, and a tower of strength. As I looked into her eyes, I saw sheer determination. I also could see her concern for us in true Mom style because she knew we were worried. Each doctor's visit became more intense, but I felt the Spirit of the Lord anchoring me to His Word. It was my only safe place of peace and strength.

Sometimes, I didn't want to speak on the phone to avoid discussing how our day went at her visits or her treatments. It was a place I wished I could escape, but all I could do was continue to find strength in the midst of my weakness through the Word of God. Trying to encourage Mom, Dad, and my sister through this process was not done by me but by the Holy Spirit, who strengthened me each day.

On one occasion, while waiting with Mom and Dad to be seen by the doctor, a young lady started conversing with me. Filled with anxiety and fear, she shared with me the issues she was facing. While she spoke, I felt the Lord tugging at my heart to pray for her. When she finished speaking, I asked if I could take her hand to pray. She agreed, and I called out to the Lord on her behalf. It was one of the most humbling experiences that changed my perspective from that day forward.

We are called to be servants of Jesus Christ and to encourage weary people who need strength through the Word of God. In Mark 10:45, Jesus said that even the Son of Man, Christ, did not come to be served but to serve and to give His life as a ransom for many. So, even in our afflictions and circumstances, Jesus wants us to reach out compassionately to pray for others as He did. In the midst of our storms, God is expecting us to praise Him. And not only praise Him but continuously be His servant by helping others.

When I prayed with that young lady, God taught me that this journey with Mom was not only about her but also for the people around us, to be a light in the midst of a storm so that all men can be drawn to Jesus Christ and bring glory to His Name!

During our travel to doctor appointments, we sang praise and worship songs that lifted our spirits. It was how we released the burdens and heaviness that would weigh us down.

In your times of experiencing the heaviness of life, I challenge you to worship the Lord Jesus. When we come to Him, honoring who He is and giving Him all the glory, He sees our hearts and lifts the load we carry. You will be lighter, so much lighter.

Chapter 4

Selfless Love

"Don't be selfish; don't try to impress others. Be humble, thinking of others as better than yourselves. Don't look out only for your own interests, but take an interest in others, too. You must have the same attitude that Jesus Christ had" – Philippians 2:3-5

It was November 24, 2019, and I was scheduled to go to work. However, I was approved for Family and Medical Leave Act (FMLA) if I needed days off to be with Mom. Working 12-hour shifts truly made a difference in being able to accompany Mom to various appointments. It was a blessing to know that I had the flexibility to support her in such a difficult time. Moving back home wasn't a hard decision but a must.

As I awoke that morning, I told Mom I wanted to stay home with her for the day. She said, "Colette, it's okay;

go to work because someone there needs you." She persisted and continued, "Your dad is here with me. Mom will be fine, but someone else needs you."

The word "self*less*" is one of many words that can describe her. If you saw Mom worried about something, it was typically 'someone' she was concerned about, whether family, friend, co-worker, or even a stranger she had just met. She exemplified the love of Christ in the way she cared for others. She never thought twice to think about others before herself. So, knowing Mom's standards and the biblical principles to which she adhered, I obeyed her and went to work that night of the 24th.

Lo and behold, there was an assignment with my name on it awaiting me. As I walked onto the unit, I was assigned to a patient in room 3; his name was Victor. He was my only patient that night as I was also charge nurse. I remember it like yesterday; the lights were dim as we usually keep them on the night shift to avoid patients from 'sundowning.' Sundowning is a state of confusion occurring in the late afternoon and lasting into the night, which also causes extreme behaviors, such as anxiety, aggression, and risk of wandering. However, it was a peaceful night.

As I knocked on my patient's door, he welcomed me in. He greeted me with a huge smile despite the condition that had hospitalized him. There was an immediate connection and bond that is still alive to this day. I felt so comfortable saying, "Can I call you Uncle Victor because I feel as if I have known you for a long time." In addition, he favored a good friend of the family, whom we called Uncle Hillocks.

Victor responded with a smile and said, "Sure!"

As I started my nursing duties, he began to share his story. He needed a heart and kidney transplant, which was information already given during report to me. He spoke about the difficult times he went through before coming to this hospital to seek more help. He said in spite of it all, he didn't lose his faith or trust in God.

I felt the presence of the Lord so heavily in the room. I was so moved that as the Lord opened my mouth, I confidently said, "The Lord is going to do something great this week before Thanksgiving! It will be a reminder each year to give God thanks for all He has done for you. To tell the world that Jesus is alive and saved your life!"

He received every word with hope in his eyes, which propelled me to ask if I could pray with him. With an open heart, he said, "Yes, I would love that!" I held his hands that night, believing the Lord for the Word spoken over his life. The 24th was the first of three shifts I had to complete, and that night, I knew the Lord used Mom to encourage me to go to work.

The second night, I went to work with the same assignment, and before I started my nursing duties, I walked in with such joy to say, "Uncle Victor, are you ready to pray and believe the Lord for what He's getting ready to do?" I touched his feet and prayed, giving God thanks for the miracle that was awaiting Victor.

For years, working as a nurse, my mother was my greatest motivator. She taught me the importance of being a servant of God. Being where I am today, I had embraced my true calling of becoming a nurse. I couldn't wait to go home and share with Mom and Dad about my patient Victor.

She was able to meet him, not in person but over the phone. He told my mom, "Thank you for letting your daughter take care of me."

As the third day approached, two days before Thanksgiving, I walked into work with expectancy and anticipation of finding out how Victor's day went. As the day shift charge nurse started giving me report on the whole unit, she immediately said, "Before I forget, Colette, tonight you are going to have to be one of the witnesses to sign the consent form for Victor to go to the operating room to receive his new heart and kidney transplant."

I was so overwhelmed with joy that honestly, I didn't know whether I should jump, run, or scream out Hallelujah! Immediately, I heard a still, small voice saying I needed to pray for Victor and the family who were at the bedside before he went into the OR.

As I approached Victor's room to receive bedside report, his wife stepped out and asked me if I would come in to pray. At that moment, I looked up, saying, Lord, thank you for confirming your Word!

I walked into the room with tears in my eyes. Uncle Victor stared steadfastly at me, and I saw the smiling faces of his dear wife and sister. I felt so compelled to share with them my mom's story about being diagnosed with cancer and how I wanted to stay home on the night I met Victor for the first time. However, I didn't stay home. My mother's selfless love of God urged her to tell me, "Go to work because someone else needs you."

The lesson learned in facing the unknown is trusting that God will take care of you when you take care of His business. Victor's miraculous story lives on today as he celebrates what the Lord has done for him every year on Thanksgiving.

As we walk with the Lord daily, He will take us to this place of self*less* love. However, we must apply the Word of God in our lives each day; then we will understand, according to Zechariah 4:6, ".... *not by might, nor by power, but by My spirit, saith the Lord of hosts.*"

Chapter 5

Answering the Call

"And the Lord came, and stood, and called as at other times, Samuel, Samuel. Then Samuel answered, Speak; for thy servant heareth" – 1 Samuel 3:10

1 Samuel chapter 3 tells of Samuel as a young man hearing the voice of God calling out to him as he was sleeping. The first two times he heard the voice, he ran to the priest Eli, whom he lived with at the temple. The third time the voice spoke, the priest perceived that it was God speaking to Samuel and instructed the young man to return to bed and, if the voice calls again, say, *"Speak; for thy servant heareth."* (1 Samuel 3:10).

Samuel's parents entrusted their son to God from early infancy to this priest named Eli, so the boy would hopefully grow up to serve God. I hope you will take the time to read the story of Samuel.

In desperate times like these, we want to hear the voice of God to direct our path. The only thing we knew to do during this trying time was to call on the name of Jesus. Even when we didn't know what to say or do, we waited to hear from the Lord. We held hands in our living room, asking for the Lord to intervene. Listening to the Lord, as Samuel did in his day, is essential.

During the process, trying to find a doctor to treat Mom was stepping into the unknown. Having in the back of our minds how aggressive this type of cancer was and, at the same time, holding onto faith.

Within a few weeks after starting chemotherapy, the next recommended treatment was radiation. However, despite the chemo treatments, the tumor size was barely shrinking. Furthermore, her weight fluctuated, and her appetite was poor. Being fearful to eat due to the side effects of the medications caused her not to keep food down. These moments of our journey were overwhelming; however, the support provided to our family during this time was a blessing.

Dr. Santi, who I call today Uncle Santi and who worked with Mom for many years, came with open arms. He assisted us with her food choices, guided us on where to go to build her immune system, and many other things. We thanked God for the good friends who supported Mom in those difficult times.

At times, it was hard to answer the phone calls. But, each person who reached out was a tower of strength sent by God to carry Mom through the most trying days of her life. Proverbs 27:17 proclaims: *"As iron sharpens iron, so one person sharpens another."* This beautiful scripture highlights the importance of the fact that, as children of God, we are never alone in this journey as servants of God. The love that poured out from countless people in our lives was overwhelming. God could use anyone in our difficult circumstances to guide, comfort, and encourage us as we leaned on the promises of God.

As children, my parents taught my sister and I the importance of serving others through their words and by example. "Serving God by serving others" is a motto the Lord gave me about how we should live daily. Jesus did not come into the world for Himself but instead for us. He said, *"I am among you as one who serves"*

(Luke 22:27). Jesus died on the cross, not for Himself but for us.

In the midst of the storm, Mom found time to bless others. I remember her receiving a monetary donation from her co-workers who were surgical physicians, fundraising on her behalf. After accepting the money, she called me into her room and said, "Colette, I want to give Sister Rose part of this money to help her put towards a used vehicle." I wanted her to remember that we had to think about the days ahead, the cost of travel, and outside appointments in NYC, and I told her as such. She replied with her faith-filled response, "Don't you worry; God will provide." Mom's faith was so big that it encouraged me to depend on the Lord for everything we needed.

Within just a few months of receiving that donation, another coworker, Mrs. Rowena, walked through the door for Thanksgiving and handed Mom an envelope with more money than she had given to Sister Rose. She stated, "Jennifer, I had a bake sale and raised this money for you and your family to help you with expenses." With tears falling, speechless, hugging each other, I felt the presence of God reminding me that He was with us in this storm.

Mom eventually turned to me and said, "See, Colette, listen to Mommy; God will always provide our needs."

During this time, we were seeking other treatment options for Mom; she couldn't handle any more chemotherapy. One day, Pastor Jones visited Mom and prayed, for it was difficult for her to attend church. While he prayed with us, the phone rang. We allowed it to go to voicemail and returned the call after his visit. On the answering machine was one of Mom's friends, a doctor. She called to inform us about another physician on Broadway in New York City who specialized in radiation treatment.

We knew that God heard our prayer that day, for that was the petition we brought before the Lord. Immediately, it was answered with one phone call we were not expecting.

Yes, Mom's mind was made up; no more chemo. This decision was made, because after multiple rounds of chemotherapy, there was no change noticed in the tumor. So, with time ticking, the Lord led us to NYC to start radiation treatment with a doctor who didn't support the use of chemotherapy. We knew very little about his background, but we believed God had opened the door. Traveling to NYC weekly became an adventure that we made the best of through the grace of God, who cared for us.

Chapter 6

The Grace of God

"And he said unto me, My grace is sufficient for thee: for my strength is made perfect in weakness. Most gladly therefore will I rather glory in my infirmities, that the power of Christ may rest upon me."
— 2 Corinthians 12:9

What is God's grace? The basic definition of grace is simply God's unmerited favor. The Hebrew word for grace is "Chen," which means favor. It is revealed 69 times in the Old Testament, making its first appearance in Genesis 6:8. It says, *"But Noah found favor in the eyes of the Lord."* How do we receive it today? It is only through Jesus. John 1:17 declares, *"For the law was given by Moses, but grace and truth came by Jesus Christ."*

2 Corinthians 12:9 shows us that Jesus' power is perfected in our weakness. Paul the Apostle, who

wrote this letter to the church in Corinth, realized the church had some issues that needed addressing. For them to overcome, he made it clear in 2 Corinthians 12:9. God's grace is sufficient in our weakness, and His strength will carry us through. Therefore, the power of Christ can truly rest upon us in our weaknesses.

No matter what the weakness is, we over come through Jesus Christ. Philippians 4:13 states, *"I can do all things through Christ which strengthen me."* On the journey, facing where each unknown road would take us, we relied on the strength of God to see us through.

One night, helping Mom prepare for bed, I could see the pain on her face as she attempted to position herself comfortably. Not wanting to burden us by seeing her hurt this way, she would say, close the door so I can rest. She prayed to the Lord for strength to continue her journey during those times. Her life was teaching mine.

With hope and faith anchoring our hearts, she started treatment on Broadway in the heart of New York City (NYC). We saw many patients coming and going and received positive testimonial reports from those who saw this doctor. We began to have hope for a chance that Mom could overcome her pancreatic cancer.

I remember Mom making a new friend named Annamaria, who also had cancer. Although both of them were going through their own trials, they looked beyond their circumstances and encouraged each other with the promises of God. The Joy of the Lord was evident in spite of the circumstances surrounding us everywhere we turned. The Bible tells us in 1 Thessalonians 5:11, *"Wherefore comfort yourselves together, and edify one another, even as also ye do."*

We took the opportunity as we drove to NYC to make it a family road trip. Dad prepared his homemade soup the night before to carry in his thermos. It was nice to have something hot to drink after we left Mom's appointment.

Mom looked forward to stopping at the clothing store across the street from the doctor's office building. We made the best of every visitation, stopping at various restaurants and enjoying NYC pizza. Dad loved to eat, and those who know me know I love to eat too, but then I blame it on Dad!

Mom made the best of every moment she could eat

without feeling nauseous. Despite the circumstances, the grace of God carried us in the most difficult times. We looked beyond our weaknesses, every thought of what could be or what the next day would bring.

Driving weekly to NYC, Daddy brought apples from the farm to Jose, who looked forward to the weekly treats. He worked in the parking garage a few blocks from the office building. The joy of the Lord swept over our souls as we took the time to serve others. Mom and Dad taught us to live this way. Doing so helped us to know we were still fulfilling our God-given purpose through this storm.

Have you ever been there before? Making the best of your circumstances? I challenge you today: if you or a loved one is experiencing sickness, look up. Pray to the Lord for strength, as Paul the Apostle told the church in Corinth. Many of us have or will face difficult times; remember that His Grace is sufficient to keep you. His Grace will allow you to have peace in the storm and boldly speak, "I can do all things through Jesus Christ that gives me strength."

I want to encourage someone today who might be going through the same situation. Don't give up! Jesus knows all about your struggle. Luke 12:7 states, *"But even the very hairs of your head are all numbered. Fear not therefore: ye are of more value than many sparrows."* He cares for you and wants you to carry everything to Him in prayer.

Chapter 7

There is a Lamb

*And Abraham said, My son, God will
provide himself a lamb for a burnt offering:
so they went both of them together"
– Genesis 22:8*

What is your sacrifice unto the Lord? John 3:16 states, *"For God so loved the world that He gave His only begotten son, that whosoever believeth in Him shall never perish but have everlasting life."* Many of us know this scripture by heart, reciting it frequently to encourage someone who doesn't believe in God. We may use it often but do not take the time to understand Jesus' true sacrifice of all humanity.

Before the foundation of the world, the Lord had me and you on His mind. He prepared the perfect sacrifice for us because He knew that a problem named "sin" would need a solution. That solution is

Jesus Christ—Who was, is, and is to come. Praise God! All of us should take the time and meditate on this one and only, paid in full sacrifice. It was the only provision to bring the world the gift of salvation.

The story of Abraham is very profound and speaks about his faith. His name is written in the Old and New Testament, speaking loudly about his faith and obeying the Lord's commands.

One of the most memorable stories is when God told Abraham to sacrifice his son as an offering unto Him. Can you imagine if the Lord spoke to you and told you to do something that seemed unimaginable to you? This proved to be God testing Abraham's faith.

As he and his son traveled to Moriah, the boy asked his father where the lamb was for the burnt offering. With great confidence, Abraham told his son, his promised child, that God would provide a lamb for the burnt offering.

As the weeks passed, traveling to NYC with Mom became a weekly routine. We kept track on the calendar when she would complete all the planned radiation treatments required. I prayed and fasted, believing and expecting that the Lord had opened this door to great results.

Mom kept a positive attitude, and Dad was the one who always encouraged Mom with scriptures to remind her of the promises of God. Although we were keenly aware that this type of cancer was difficult to fight, our faith never failed.

However, I did feel as if I was in the middle of the ocean, holding onto an anchor to keep me from being tossed to and fro by the storm's waves. Seeking the face of God, especially at night, was my safe haven. The Word was my keeper. It encouraged me to stand firm on my faith when sleepless nights and tears overwhelmed me.

As December approached, the days went by swiftly. Mom was scheduled to do a repeat PET scan because her last radiation treatment was approaching. With hope in our hearts, we believed it would be well.

Following the PET scan, we made our way over to the doctor's office on Broadway, a few blocks from where the scan was done. While we waited for the nurse to call Mom's name, the atmosphere was tense, filled with anxiety, hoping to get a good report that things were turning in the right direction.

Dad stayed in the waiting room while I accompanied Mom, holding her hand. As we entered the room, we were first greeted by the doctor's assistant (his son who worked with him). The countenance on his face spoke before he ever said a word, giving me a feeling that I wouldn't wish on anyone.

He began to speak and said, "Mrs. Atkinson, I am so sorry. The cancer has spread to your liver, and there are multiple lesions on it. The tumor on the pancreas is the same size with little to no improvement."

Sitting there with tears in my eyes and hopelessness starting to creep into my heart, I looked up at my mother. With a sincere look of peace on her face, she said, "It is well, doc. It is well."

We called for my dad to come into the room. The primary care doctor explained in detail what his assistant told us. He showed us the imaging and stated, "There's nothing we can do, but there is another doctor we would like to recommend that can infuse chemo directly into the liver, as a last resort to try to kill the cancer cells invading the liver and pancreas."

With a serious expression, Mom said emphatically, "No more chemo!" And then peacefully, she stated again, "It is well, doc. It is well." She thanked him for all he had done and told him it was all in the Lord's hands.

As we drove back home, there wasn't much talking, just the radio playing soothing worship music from the family broadcast station. Remembering the city street lights and the rushing traffic around us, we sat silently in our seats. My heart was overwhelmed, but I could only imagine how my Mom and Dad felt at that point.

Trying to stay strong for everyone was all that I knew to do. Looking up to the Lord, I finally broke the silence and said, "She shall live and not die to declare the works of the Lord!" It was the only encouraging Word I could give Mom that day.

Reaching home two hours later, Mom went to her room to lie down. Dad and I stayed in the upstairs living room. We both looked at each other as if to say, "What do we do now?"

As I pondered the day's events, I heard a soft voice

whisper, "There is a ram." I immediately remembered the scripture about Abraham, who took his son to offer a sacrifice unto the Lord as God instructed him to. With this being the new vision, we continued the journey by faith. Despite the bad news, hope ignited within my soul, remembering the Good News of Jesus Christ!

With hope arising again, I remember picking up my phone to call Dr. Santi to give him the update and let him know that Mom desires no more chemo. He then asked us to contact one of his doctor friends, Dr. Dela.

It was the beginning of meeting three souls that impacted our lives immensely. Dr. Dela was the first of them all. I felt Jesus' presence that night. It didn't feel like the end, but there was perhaps another way. Although it was after 9 pm, I immediately called the doctor's office and left a message on the answering machine.

The next day, a call came, bringing a glimmer of light in the darkness. They could schedule Mom for an appointment. In that moment, we felt a surge of hope and joy, as if the unknown wasn't a dead end, but a tunnel with daylight at the end.

Chapter 8

I Am the Way

"Jesus saith unto him, I am the way, the truth, and the life; no man cometh unto the Father, but by me" — John 14:6

Have you ever found yourself at a crossroad, unsure of which path to take? In those moments, remember, there is always hope. It's the hope that Jesus Christ, who came and died for me and you, brings. He is the perfect sacrifice, the one who comforts, guides, and leads us through the darkest of times.

The lovely Psalm 34:4-6 states, *"I sought the Lord, and he heard me, and delivered me from all my fears. They looked unto him, and were lightened: and their faces were not ashamed. This poor man cried, and the Lord heard him, and saved him out of all his troubles."*

During the hardest moment, when fear crept in, we

called upon the name of the Lord Jesus. Sometimes, you may not have any words, but can I tell you that tears are a language the Heavenly Father understands. Another beautiful scripture, Psalm 56:8-9 says, *"Thou tellest my wanderings: put thou my tears into thy bottle: are they not in thy book? When I cry unto thee then shall mine enemies turn back: this I know; for God is for me."*

The Psalmist, David, trusts that God is for him and that God will not allow his enemies to overtake him. He is reflecting on God's promises in times of trouble. Therefore, as Christians, we also must reflect on and recall what Jeremiah said in Lamentations chapter 3: God sees all our pain.

Recalling the promises of God helps us on our journey. No matter the circumstances, there is always victory in the name of Jesus. Jesus is the way to life and truth. He is the way to gain peace in times of trouble, joy in times of sadness, relief from pain in times of sorrow, and laughter when you're feeling down.

Despite the desperation lurking in the background, we stepped out in faith and scheduled Mom for her next appointment. Remembering the soft voice that had spoken, "There is a ram," I realized I didn't get the complete revelation. But I knew with confidence that ultimately, Jesus is the Lamb. The perfect sacrifice.

The time came for Mom to make her appointment in Stanfordville, NY. As we drove, we experienced the beautiful scenery of the farms with cows and horses trotting around the country homes. Seeing God's creation of nature helped soothe Mom on our journey. She said, "One day when I get better, I want to go back home to my country, the Island of Jamaica."

The doctor and his secretary were pleasant and welcoming as we walked into the office. Although Mom was becoming weak, we kept the faith that there would be something that could at least build her immune system to fight off the cancer cells. Hope remained in our hearts, although we continued to face the unknowns of tomorrow.

The doctor reviewed Mom's labs, PET scan, MRI imaging, and detailed reports from the beginning to that point in time. He told us that he wished he had been able to see her in the beginning before she received the chemotherapy. However, he persevered by setting up a plan to infuse her with IV Vitamin C and other homeopathic medicine, hoping to restore the damaged cells within her body. We welcomed this type of treatment, and so did Mom.

Her first two infusions truly helped and increased strength in her body. Thankfully, she was able to keep down her food and liquids. She also received an injection for pain, which helped her through this process.

The journey was challenging, but the grace of God showed her favor with her beautiful co-workers, making a way to get into appointments quicker than usual for anything she needed. Dr. Elmosly, Zoha, Cherry, Stern, and Zonick...her sweet manager Ann Marie, Aunty Chicky, Rowena, Wendy, Baboo, JR, and many others stood by her side. We never lacked anything needed, and indeed, we thank God for it all.

The journey of facing the unknown continued. Dr. Dela introduced us to one of his friends, Ron Buffone, who specializes in natural health and medicine. As it turned out, Ron, who I call my brother today, was the next Godsend we met the same week.

When we left our first appointment with Dr. Dela, we called Ron as we drove home. Our hearts were sincere in seeking help. He answered the phone with a warm tone and zeal to help as he listened to Mom's story. After we explained Mom's diagnosis, he wanted to see her immediately.

As we walked through his door that same day, with a smile on his face, he greeted us with a question, "Are you believers?"

We happily said, "Yes, we are!"

He began by telling us his testimony of how he started getting into herbal medicine. (To read more about Ron, please see the last chapter on "Testimonies of Jennifer Atkinson.)" He gave Mom instructions on a specific diet plan and supplied herbal teas for her to drink daily. He also recommended therapies that would help improve Mom's health.

We had one of the most life-changing experiences during our first visit with Ron. Before laying out the plan to help her, he prayed. He thanked God for sending Mom so that he could help her in whatever capacity the Lord saw fit, all for His Glory.

Oh, what joy filled our souls! Hope continued to be

renewed while facing the unknown. God sent his faithful servants to be a blessing, reminding us that there is still hope and we need each other to survive.

After meeting Ron that day, he became a part of our journey in *facing the unknown*. There was a reassurance every step along the way that made it clear: if we follow the "I Am" way, we will make it all the way. This firsthand experience showed us that the Anchor still holds when we put our trust in Jesus.

Although Ron realized Mom's health was deteriorating slowly, he saw hope, faith, and life beyond what his human eyes could see. He saw a fighter in Mom that was beyond words. He stood by us with faith, knowing that nothing is impossible with God. He shared scriptures with great joy as he gave us remedies to assist with Mom's quality of life.

One of Ron's recommendations was for Mom to receive a natural cleanser to help eliminate waste in her colon. This led us to a third beautiful soul named Crystal. I call her "Crystal anointed," a true blessing from the Lord surrounded by His glorious presence. Beautiful Crystal, full of faith, zeal, and the Holy Spirit, opened her door with joy from helping to save souls. As we continued following every step the Lord led us to, we saw God's hand in the midst of it all.

Within two days, the Lord opened the door for our visits with Dr. Dela, Ron, and Crystal. Each of them helped us see hope while facing the unknown. Who could it be but God? We saw the favor of God through servants of God. Their minds were not fixed on money but on seeking the truth and looking for a solution through natural health and wellness, the way we felt God intended it to be.

As we walked through Crystal's door on that cold winter day, she greeted us with a beaming smile and a hug. We were total strangers, but a family in Christ was found that day. I believe she already knew we were Christians because she immediately shared her testimony on how the Lord led her to become a colonic therapist. The trials and tribulations she overcame by Jesus Christ propelled her into being who she is today and helping others overcome sicknesses that tend to hinder many from functioning normally.

Just like Ron, she asked if we could pray first before she started any treatment for Mom. With great joy, we said ardently, "YES!" After she prayed, the Lord showed her, in an open vision, a gift with a big bow in front of Mom. She couldn't explain it, but we received it in our hearts that Mom had a special gift awaiting her.

There is a joy that only comes through knowing Jesus and believing that He will guide our steps while facing our unknowns. The Bible says in Psalms 37:4-5, *"Take delight in the Lord, and he will give you your heart's desires. Commit everything you do to the Lord. Trust him, and he will help you."*

So, let us be encouraged to tell God what we need and thank Him for all He has done. It's pleasing unto Him when we believe He is who He says He is, the "I Am the way."

Chapter 9

Are You Saved?

"Now when they heard this, they were pricked in their heart, and said unto Peter and to the rest of the apostles, Men and brethren, what shall we do? And Peter said unto them, Repent, and be baptized every one of you in the name of Jesus Christ for the remission of sins, and ye shall receive the gift of the Holy Ghost" — Acts 2:37–38

Before Jesus ascended into Heaven, He promised He would send the Comforter, the Holy Spirit. He said to his disciples, *"Nevertheless I tell you the truth; It is expedient for you that I go away: for if I go not away, the Comforter will not come unto you; but if I depart I will send him unto you"* (John 16:7).

This incredible promise is seen through scripture, reminding us that Jesus is coming back, but the great news is that we can experience Him right now. Today!

The book of Acts is a book of action, speaking about the promise of the gift we shall receive. Peter makes it clear, as we see in the referenced scripture for this chapter (please remember to take the time to go back into the scriptures and read them fully so you can receive a deeper understanding of the context), that when they heard the people speaking in tongues as the Spirit gave them utterance, men from all over were pricked in their hearts as Peter spoke boldly about what they had witnessed. Peter gave them the plan of salvation after being asked, "What shall I do to be saved?"

As you read this through, it's my heart's desire that you experience God's rich presence and have your heart pricked, just like those men in Acts 2. They wanted to experience the power of the Holy Spirit within them so they could do great things as the Lord promised before He returned. Receiving the power of the Holy Spirit gives you the strength to overcome the storms of life when you are weak.

With great confidence and faith, I knew that giving my life to God on January 11, 2015, was the best decision I ever made. Being filled with His Spirit, with the evidence of speaking in tongues, my life was never the same.

We sing a song in church titled "Fill My Cup Lord." The song's first few lines say, "Like the woman at the well, I was seeking, for things that could not satisfy, but then I heard my savior speaking, draw from the well that never shall run dry." This song speaks volumes; as a young woman, I was seeking things in this world to satisfy me. As I drew closer to Him, I felt the Lord changing my worldly desires into desiring to know Him more as my personal Savior.

When the storm came amid our family, the Holy Spirit kept us. The Holy Spirit made the way when our backs were against the wall. Yes, it was Jesus!! We touched the hem of His garment in a desperate time for Mom, which caused our eyes to look at Him.

Have you ever been in that place…when you turned to a friend, family member, or the doctor, and no one was there to help? Well, there is a man named Jesus who can, for in Him dwells the fullness of the Godhead. He is the image of the invisible God. The Apostle Paul goes into detail in Colossians 1:19 proclaiming that Jesus is the Supreme Being and has the authority to bring redemption and reconciliation so that all humanity can be saved from sin.

His grace and mercies kept us through the raging storm that tried to consume us. His loving arm raised us from the miry clay, which could have caused our faith to fail. He planted our feet on the Rock of Salvation to stand when everything else was sinking.

From a young age, my parents taught me and my sister the importance of knowing the Lord. During these difficult times, we are grateful for the humble beginnings that never left our hearts. Mom was thankful that although chemotherapy and radiation didn't help, there was still hope in Jesus. The hands that touched her were God-sent; no matter what came her way, she was in the hands of our Savior, Jesus.

It was in 1996 when Mom accepted Jesus Christ as her Lord and Savior and was baptized. Her life was never the same, and she lived knowing that His Anchor still holds no matter the storms.

One day, I remember seeing Mom sitting up in her bed sewing her decorative pillows. She looked up and saw the countenance on my face; concerned, she said with confidence, "Colette, mommy is going to be fine, and I know because the Lord has brought me a mighty long way." She went on to say, "I can remember when I first came to Canada from Jamaica. With no legal documents, my visa was getting ready to expire. I prayed daily for the Good Lord to send me a good husband. And the Lord sent your dad, whom I didn't know for long before we married. And when I met your grandfather (dad's father), he told your dad, *that's the one.* Your Grandfather paid for my dress, the ring, and the entire wedding. It didn't cost me a dime."

She continued, "I can recall working at this factory, where it was mostly immigrants who didn't have any documents to work. One day, I wasn't feeling well and decided to stay home. The next day, a friend of mine called me and said, 'Jennifer, whatever side of the bed you slept on last night, go back and sleep on it again because yesterday immigration came and swept out everyone without legal documents and deported them back to Jamaica.' It was then that I realized even more that God was with me."

She boldly shared her testimony that day, reassuring me that Jesus is with us and knows everything best.

"Don't you worry, my child," she said. The smile on her face settled my mind, and I knew Jesus was with us for sure. Although I had planned on how I believed things should turn out, I had to yield to the Lord for strength daily to lean not unto my own understanding but acknowledge Him in all my ways.

As weeks and months passed by, it became much harder to see Mom go through the process. Her body started retaining fluid, her legs became weaker, and she couldn't mobilize as she usually would. One day, Mom's longtime friend, Mrs. Carmen, who was such a blessing, came by the house to visit. She was not too hearty in health herself, but she made every effort to stop by and help us care for Mom, giving her baths and assisting her to bed.

Mom's gait became weaker and weaker as the weeks passed by. Our family doctor, Dr. Anwar, was very transparent and made it clear one day that things were not looking good. We held on to Jesus in our hearts but knew she was ready to go home to the Lord by how Mom was talking.

On this particular day, Mom needed a wheelchair to leave the house for her doctor's appointment. As I watched her sitting in the recliner chair receiving her treatment, she was so weak. Nevertheless, she pushed through her weakness just for us. She was tired, weary, and ready but persevered because of her family and friends. Somehow, while leaving the appointment with Dr. Dela, I knew this was the last time Mom would be seeing him.

I remember coming home from work the morning of Christmas Eve and walking up the stairs; I saw Dad and Mom in the living room. Dad's face was lined with concern. I asked him what was wrong. He replied, "I think we need to take Mom to the hospital. She's so frail and can barely walk."

I looked at Mom; her face was pale. "Mom, we need to go to the hospital just to be safe."

She was checked in upon arriving at the emergency room; blood work and vital signs were completed first. When the results of her blood work returned, the nurse practitioner came in the room and said Mom's hemoglobin level was very low, and her kidney function was slightly elevated.

With hope in my heart, I still believed that God could

turn all this around. Turning to the Lord for strength, I encouraged Mom not to lose hope, "You will make it through."

She decided to receive a blood transfusion, and on the same day, she was discharged. When we returned home, she said, "Colette, I'm glad we went because I really needed that blood."

The week went by, and it was the toughest time for Mom. Due to her inability to walk up the stairs, we prepared the basement area as her bedroom. Thank God it was already set up as a bedroom area. Mom loved decorating and prepared an area for anyone who came to stay over. This area for her guests became her new bedroom, where we lay beside her at night.

New Year's Eve was another time we went back to the hospital to be seen. The doctors ran more tests to see what was decreasing her hemoglobin level. They realized she had developed a stomach ulcer, which was most likely caused by the radiation.

The greatest gift was being with my mom at her bedside and seeing my church family by our side. Working in the health field, one can relate to the fact that it's not always an easy road being alone as a patient admitted to the hospital. It was a privilege to know I could be her servant; with the help of family and friends, we were kept a long way.

She was grateful to have excellent nurses at Midhudson Regional Hospital in Poughkeepsie, NY. All of them who cared for Mom took great joy in caring for her.

On January 1st, my sister, dad, brother-in-law, niece and nephew, and a few other relatives were there to visit Mom. She took that opportunity, in her pain, to express her wishes to everyone in the room. We all cried and embraced each other, but we still hoped that all would turn out well for Mom.

The doctor came in one day to have a family meeting. He let us know that there was nothing more they could do. Dad was more understanding, but my sister and I believed for a miracle. She refused hospice care but preferred that we take her home and continue to care for her and receive assistance as needed by rehab.

On Sunday, January 19th, 2020, the morning came; I opened my eyes laying beside Mom. Her eyes were already open, staring at me. With a firm look, she said, "I'm done; I'm ready." I didn't want to receive it, even though deep within my heart, I knew she was ready to go home to be with the Lord. I heard the Lord say, if we take her to the hospital today, she won't be coming back home.

With this, I remember calling a brother in Christ, Jovan, who I knew would pray with me earnestly for a change. He was there within 10 minutes of calling him, but with the look on his face, I knew he had seen beyond what I could see.

I repeated the scripture from Psalm 118:17, "I shall not die but live, and declare the works of the Lord," to Mom, and I then told her to repeat it. In that very moment, when I could have called the ambulance, I kept stretching the faith I had, believing for a miracle.

She continued fighting for us, her family, and her friends, but the next day, we had no choice but to call for an ambulance so she could be admitted to the hospital. Our hearts were overwhelmed, but yet not in despair. Jesus, the Anchor to our souls, allowed us to stand strong.

We all have an expected end date to leave this world. Have you ever thought about it? Or do you try to avoid thinking about it because you don't want to face it? I ask these questions because they are the same questions I asked myself. I never liked to think about or imagine leaving my loved ones behind or even thinking of death at all. However, as the years have gone by and I continued growing in the Lord, it has opened my eyes more to what matters in and after this life.

I implore you, if you are not saved, consider Jesus today! Jesus came to die for you and me so that we can have life and have it more abundantly in Him until He returns as promised unto us. Hebrews 9:27-28 says, *"And as it is appointed unto men once to die, but after this the judgment: So, Christ was once offered to bear the sins of many; and unto them that look for him shall he appear the second time without sin unto salvation."*

Chapter 10

I Saw the Lord

"In the year that king Uzziah died I saw also the Lord sitting upon a throne, high and lifted up, and his train filled the temple"
— Isaiah 6:1

The signs were evident that Mom's time to leave this earth was near. Leading up to the last days before Mom's admission to the hospital on January 20th, 2020, I looked back and remembered the many comments she made in the house to Dad, my sister, and me. She spoke in parables, not directly telling us her time was near, but to give us time to allow the Lord to show us that His will must be done.

One day, looking out the window in her living room upstairs, she said, "Colette, you better tough up because it's going to get worse." Mommy saw my tears, although I tried to hide them. Even so, her faith and boldness amazed me. She never allowed her circumstances to move her from the firm foundation.

Mom was truly a warrior, for in the weakest moment of her life, she yielded to the will of God. She never complained about her sickness but continued to say, "It is well." Dad called family and friends on the phone to come and see Mom because she wouldn't be with us much longer. No matter, somehow, deep within my soul, my faith was so BIG I didn't believe the Lord would take her. Instead, I was waiting for the miraculous!

The night went by as Mom laid down so comfortably; her face was glowing, as many said as they came to visit. She never required much pain medication, as the doctors suggested. Mom would say to her doctor colleagues at work, "Doc, I'm a cheap date." Meaning she doesn't drink alcohol, nor does she like taking pain medication.

The hospital room and hallway were crowded with friends and family. Looking around me, I said, "Lord, is this really happening?" But during this time, I saw the Lord keeping our family. Our faith remained alive in the most devastating time of our life.

Before we knew it, the 21st of January was here, and she lay peacefully in bed. There was no sign of pain or distress, but peace engulfed the atmosphere. Prayer and worship empowered us through our church family, which always stood by us. As the night was drawing nigh, Sister Rose and I asked Mom if we could give her a bath; with a soft voice, she agreed and said, "Let this be the last." Reflecting on her humility, strength, and endurance on this journey still amazes me.

As stated before, the nursing and hospital staff were so caring and allowed us to stay with Mom at all times. At night, I took on the role of being beside her because I knew it would be hard for my sister with her children and for Dad. We worked together, ensuring she was well cared for as she always did for her family, friends, and even strangers.

I laid in the recliner that night after bathing her; it was approximately 2 am. Tears flushed my face, and I sat beside her and cried from the depths of my heart for the Lord to speak to me. At that moment, I saw my mother open her eyes and look intently at me. She said with a firm voice, "Stop crying." I didn't understand why she would say this to me. How could my mother expect me to stop crying. How?

Have you ever been there? Someone so dear to your heart like a mother, a loved one, a friend? Deep within my soul, as she said those two words, there was a confidence of great hope in her voice as I stared into her eyes. There is only one way I can describe what I saw in the Spirit; it was as if she had a glimpse of Heaven. She laid still in her Heavenly Father's arms with no sadness but with great hope that her redeemer lives.

I remember it like it was yesterday, on January 22, 2020, as we surrounded Mom's bed. It seemed so surreal as I watched her breathing become shallower; I started to say within me, "Lord, is this it? Are you really taking her home?"

I played worship music from Pandora on my phone; I put it close by so she could hear. The last song was "It's Not Over Until God Says It's Over." I remember it well. I turned to my sister, as she was hysterically crying, and said, "Kristina, don't you believe? It's not over! The Lord is going to do a miracle!" My faith was so big that I believed God could do it!

Someone else said, "Colette, it's finished!" But I turned and repeated the same thing to her. "Don't you believe that Jesus can do it?" Even though I knew on some level that God's will must be done, nothing hindered my faith! I wanted to see God physically heal her before my eyes because He is able!

As my Pastor, Rohan Richards, walked through the doors to comfort and pray with our family, he said, "To be absent in the body is to be present with God." It was hard to accept or even comprehend, but the words spoken by those around us never left my mind.

At that moment, my faith felt like it had ended, but deep within, I knew the Lord's Anchor still holds. I knew God was holding our hands through it all, but it hurt so badly. In the midst of my pain, I looked at my mom lying so peacefully and remembered her last words to me, "Stop crying." I didn't understand how she could expect me not to, but I knew there was a light ahead that I couldn't see as I continued facing the unknown.

As the nurse caring for Mom walked into the room to confirm she had stopped breathing, I asked if my sister and I could care for her body. She gladly said yes as she went to do the preliminary protocols—calling the doctor and the funeral home. We anointed her body and prayed before leaving her room. It brought us comfort and a sense of peace.

The year my dearest mother, Jennifer Ivoree Atkinson, passed away, I saw the Lord. I've seen things from a different perspective than before. The Lord reminded me of the dreams my mother shared with me. One in particular comes to mind. Mom explained she was driving her vehicle, and her eyes were closed. While driving, she tried hard to open her eyes, but they wouldn't open. Despite her eyes being closed, her vehicle didn't crash, and she safely reached her destination. When she could finally open her eyes, the car was gone.

On the day Mom went home to be with the Lord, He reminded me of this dream she shared. The vehicle represented her journey on this earth, walking by faith. As believers, we walk by faith and not by sight, as declared in 2 Corinthians 5:7. When the Lord took her, her eyes were opened, but not to the physical journey on this earth. Her spiritual eyes were open to her eternal home.

At the end of our journey on this earth, our souls will return to the only true and living God. Mom received her healing, her spiritual healing, one that is greater than the physical.

"Hear, O Israel: The LORD our God is one Lord: And thou shalt love the Lord thy God with all thine heart, and with all thy soul, and with all thy might. And these words, which I command these this day, shall be in thine heart: And thou shalt teach them diligently unto thy children, and shalt walk of them when thou sittest in thine house, and when thou walkest by the way, and when thou liest down, and when thou risest up." – Deuteronomy 6:4-7

Let our hearts love the Lord all the days of our lives as we pass this love down to our children so we can experience the everlasting joy of the Lord.

Chapter 11

A Collection of Testimonies

"And they overcame him by the blood of the Lamb, and by the word of their testimony; and they loved not their lives unto the death"
— Revelation 12:11

At the end of her journey, Jennifer impacted many lives and fulfilled her God-given purpose. Those who knew her experienced a woman with a servant's heart. Those who never knew her could see the evidence of a life well lived at her home-going service and, I believe, within the pages of this book. She was a dedicated hard worker at Vassar Brothers Medical Center in Poughkeepsie, New York, for 39 years, where she retired.

Throughout the years of her life, many lives were touched. My eyes were opened to this at my mom's funeral as I walked up to the podium to sing a tribute song, "Wind Beneath My Wings," as requested by her. I couldn't believe the amount of people that filled the sanctuary. I could hear her voice saying, *Colette, continue the work, for my work is finished, but we must go on.*

Many testimonies were spoken at the service, and most importantly, many realized that fulfilling our purpose is truly what God has called us for at the end of the day. Many said she was too young to die, but a life fulfilled on this earth by God is indeed the goal. Lives were transformed. Not only while she was living but also after her death. Her legacy still lives on.

I want to challenge you to write down how to live an impactful life. What is your purpose? And what will they say at your funeral? As I saw lives changed, I pray you will as well. I hope you accomplish all that God has called you to be and fulfill before you leave this world. No matter what circumstances you are going through, trust the Lord.

How can you trust Him in your circumstances? First, you must acknowledge and believe Jesus is the Savior of the world, who died for your sins. Repent, be baptized in the name of Jesus, and the gift of the Holy Ghost you will receive as written in Acts 2:38. Once you surrender your life, having faith becomes easier as you go. You will learn to trust Him in your circumstances. Will it always be easy? No, it won't be, but I can confidently promise that the Anchor still holds, and He will see you through.

Facing the unknown at the beginning of our journey wasn't easy, and it will not be easy for you. But stand still and see the salvation of the Lord.

At the end of Mom's fulfilled life, she was an overcomer by the blood of the Lamb and by the word of her testimony. She lived her life as a servant but could say with great boldness, "It is well with my soul."

The Bible gives many scriptures that share the story of God-fearing people whose testimonies caused them to be overcomers through Jesus Christ. The Bible says in Revelation 12:10-11, *"And I heard a loud voice saying in heaven, Now is come salvation, and strength, and the kingdom of our God, and the power of his Christ: for the accuser of the brethren is cast down, which accused them before our God day and night. And they overcame him by the blood of the lamb, and by the word of their testimony; and they loved not their lives unto the death."*

We see here that Satan, the father of lies, is the accuser of the brethren. He wants to seduce God's children with the forces of darkness. But we have good news today.

Salvation has come! Now, we can obtain strength and power from God through the cross of Calvary! His blood and the word of our testimony make us overcomers! Our precious Savior, Jesus Christ, paid it all for you and me.

Have you ever gone to the store to pay a bill in full? There's a feeling you get when you know you're free from the debt. Well, God's forgiveness is better than that! We have a blessed assurance that our debt of sin is paid in full through salvation, and nothing can separate us from Christ Jesus.

This book wouldn't be complete without incorporating a few testimonies from others who were a part of Mom's life. As you read each one, I pray you will find strength, be empowered in your circumstances, and have the peace of God all the days of your life. Proverbs 27:17 proclaims, *"As iron sharpens iron, so one person sharpens another."* This simple statement has been a calling for all of God's servants to understand that no one is alone. We are iron sharpeners. Today, be sharpened as you read each line upon line in Jesus' name.

TESTIMONIES FROM THOSE WHO KNEW JENNIFER IVOREE ATKINSON

It was in the early '80s when I had the good fortune of meeting Jennifer. From the first day, I noticed the flow of positivity and optimism, along with her smile. She had a consistently happy-go-lucky type of demeanor. She was always helping others and facilitating the work around her. It didn't take long for her to be liked and loved by everyone. Her smile and attitude became her trademark.

She made it easy for her peers and supervisors to approach her about changes in assignments in the schedule. We all could count on Jennifer when the need arose. In the mid-80s, she was blessed with the pregnancy of a daughter…a pride she carried for the rest of her life. She taught her about family and cultural values with a special kind of Mother's Love.

Over the years, Jennifer stepped up to learn and adjust to the new incoming technologies. She received all the required qualifications as a first-class surgical technologist. She accumulated a lot of experience that helped her handle challenging cases.

Jennifer's faithful hope was part of her daily living, giving her the strength to endure all the obstacles and surprises life threw at her. She remained strong and determined to the last of her days. She had a life well lived, a role model to those around her; the way she loved and cared for others was her legacy. All this transferred to her daughter Colette, carrying all those special values to share with family, friends, and her patients. She is proud of her mother's life and will continue to be a witness to Jennifer's legacy.

May our Creator keep her in eternal peace.

— *Dr. Santi*

———————◄•

I am writing this testimonial for my dear sister, friend, and colleague, the late Jennifer Atkinson. I met Jennifer in July 2001 when I started working at Vassar Brothers Medical Center in Poughkeepsie, NY. My encounter with 'Jen,' as I always call her, was pleasant, professional, and respectful. Over the years, we have been working together with other charities to provide support and assistance to needy families both financially and by providing services such as food and clothing.

Jennifer was an angel sent by God to carry out a mission in this world, and she did it without hesitation. She organized clothing drives, collected furniture for needy families, and was involved in a host of other humanitarian activities. She would cook food daily and bring it to work for everyone to eat. We became very close friends, and at some point, I was part of her family. She was caring, especially to her patients. She was compassionate and a wonderful mother, grandmother, and wife. She will surely be missed. However, her legacy didn't end…her beautiful, loving, caring, and compassionate daughter, Colette Atkinson, continues her journey. May her memory be a blessing to humanity.

From a dear friend,
— *Mr. Baboucarr Gaye*

———————◄•

Psalm 122:1 says, *"I was glad when they said unto me, Let us go into the house of the Lord.."* Psalm 16:11 says, *"Thou wilt shew me the path of life: in thy presence is fulness of joy; at thy right hand there are pleasures for evermore."* Sister Jennifer reminds me of these two scriptures; her life speaks out loud to me and has impacted my life in many ways.

I remember the times she would call and ask if I was home. She wanted to drop something off for me and the kids. One Christmas, I was surprised by her gift of plenty for one of my daughters and grandchildren. The gifts kept coming; it was so much that it overflowed like milk and honey. We were all surprised and grateful and the surprises kept coming. Sometimes, she would call to ask if I was ok and if I needed anything.

She loved people and loved to care for others. She was one of a kind ... a gem. She was Christ-like. She talked the talk, and she walked the walk. During her journey with cancer, she fought a good fight like a brave soldier in the army for Christ; not fearing the enemy of cancer, she put her faith and trust in God. She never wavered or doubted God's presence in her life. She looked cancer in the eyes fearlessly, bustled up her boots of righteousness, and marched on no matter the circumstances. How she lived proves that she has won the victory in Christ Jesus and defeated the cancer giant. Her spirit will forever live on. She has gained the bravery of excellency in her Lord and Savior, Jesus Christ.

There are many more attributes about her that speak volumes in my life. The gift of plenty keeps coming from Sis Jennifer. I remember getting a call from her once, and she asked me if I had work. I told her no, and she asked me what my pay would have been. She called me again within a day or two and asked if I was home; she wanted to drop something off for me. To my surprise, it was an envelope with the pay I would have received if I had worked.

Another time, I got a call from her; she and Bro Keith, her husband, came by my house during her sickness. She sat on the bottom of the steps and handed me an envelope. Open it, she said. It was $1,000 in cash! I was so shocked I cried and asked what I did to deserve this. She replied, I love you, and you are my sister. I could hardly climb the stairs. My knees were weak in shock at what was handed to me. There were plenty of times I literally had to hide from her because the gift of plenty kept coming.

Before she got sick, she would call me to come by her house to give me some apples. She made sure she picked the best and biggest apples in the box! When she gave me food from her garden, Bro Keith would ensure it was the best without any spots or blemishes. When she gave, she did it with a clean heart without expecting anything back in return.

I could say so many things about Sister Jennifer; the list goes on and on. If I should express all the good things about her, there would be no room for others to testify about her. I certainly can say gratitude is a must, and she will forever be in my heart. I will always love my Sister Jennifer.

— *Sister Rose Atkinson*
————————◂•

I met Jennifer, also known as "Moy," some years ago at a friend's 50th birthday celebration. Then, a short period later, I met up with her on an Alaskan Cruise. On this occasion, my spirit wanted to be as close to her as possible. She possessed a special aura that captivated me. From that time, we became very close friends. She was like a sister to me and was interested in my welfare. She was such a caring, kind-hearted person. A beautiful soul she was.

She was a tower of strength when my husband got seriously ill. Moy would call me daily, no matter how busy she was caring for her sick patients. She consistently made time for me amid a busy schedule to contact me and see how my husband was doing. Moy would go the extra mile by supplying me with Pampers and other necessities that she deemed helpful for my husband's well-being.

She was a special friend provided by God for me. Moy was always there to encourage me during my husband's long illness. The last conversation she and I had was in her garden. She picked some fever grass that she had planted. She told me, Boil this for Errol and make sure he drinks it; this fever grass will keep him calm.

Moy will always have a special place in my heart for her selfless giving and caring for others. May her soul rest in Eternal Peace."

Love Always,
— *Sister Mitsy*

————————◄•

It is indeed an honor to give a testimony of Jennifer. I first met Jen in June of 2016 when I joined the Vassar Brothers Medical Center Operating Room team. She was this very kind and gentle soul, so friendly and compassionate. She worked the evening shift with me and was ready to jump in any case. She loved her job, was dedicated, and hardly ever called out. Jen and I clicked, and as I got to know her more personally, I learned that she was selfless and even more compassionate outside of work.

Being that we both were immigrants, we looked at things very differently. We talked a lot about how wasteful the American culture was. As we pondered how to recycle some of the waste, I realized Jen was way ahead of me. She was affiliated with some friends at the Rotary Club and often went dumpster diving to retrieve medical equipment that would eventually be shipped to 3rd world countries that needed them. To Jen, nothing went to waste, and I admired that.

Like me, it was not unusual to find Jen buying things she didn't need at a garage sale, but she always knew somebody else who needed them. At Thanksgiving, if Jen wasn't working, she would cook and make a plate for everyone else working that day. In the Fall, Jen brought apples for everyone in the OR.

On a personal note, I cannot forget how Jen helped me when my brother and his three young sons arrived in the US and were living with me. Not only did Jen supply me with lots of apples, but she also made some arrangements with Panera Bread, and I would get a supply of pastries every week. She would say, Connie, take more bread. The boys need to eat! Evidently, she did this for many because she often spoke of the people she was reaching out to who needed help.

Jen was a true face of compassion, a real down-to-earth person, and very involved in the community. Besides her family, the passing of Jen was a terrible loss for all of us co-workers and friends who remember her for her warmth, generosity of spirit, and talent as a surgical technologist.

May her soul continue to rest in peace.
— *Sister Connie*

—————————◄•

Have you ever used the word 'self*less*ness'? Maybe someone has done an act of kindness or a good deed, and you would say it was selfless. But can you imagine a person whose entire life is about giving, caring, sharing, and loving? Not an act...but a lifestyle of daily living?

This brings me to take this opportunity to share my friend Jennifer with you. This woman not only gave you her time, love, and compassion but went far above all you could ever think or imagine. She gave beyond understanding. She gave beyond measure. Her giving has changed the lives of God's people forever.

Jennifer gave without reservations. She gave when her basket was full, when it was half full, and when it was almost empty. Some could ask how one can give out of nothing. Don't ask me! All I can say is that her

Godly love and kindness kept that basket recycled, regenerated, and fully restored.

So, back to the word 'selflessness,' have you looked at the definition? Well, I found out it's not an adjective or a verb. It's actually a noun. Honestly, I didn't know that. The most accurate form of the word is a person, and her name has left an indelible mark on our lives. Oh, my friend, the meaning is JENNIFER! Look it up, and you will see.

Never has a life been so loved and appreciated than a life lived so selfless. Simply amazing!

— *Sister Lorna*

Jennifer worked as a nurse aid on one of the Medical Floors at Vassar Brothers Medical Center. Jen was always looking for new ways to help people, so when a new job was posted for labor and delivery, she applied for it and got it. This is how I met her, as a co-worker in Labor and Delivery, and we soon became fast friends.

When I think of Jen (and I think of her often), the things that jump out at me are all words of praise. Jen was hard-working, selfless, always upbeat, in a good mood, and proud of her culture and religion. She always told us stories of Jamaica and her uncle, a lobster fisherman. While we always treated lobster as a delicacy, she said that she ate so much of it in Jamaica that she couldn't even look at it anymore. I used to call her 'Island Girl'.

I worked on the 3-11 shift. When I arrived at work and saw who was on duty, I knew it would be a good night if Jen was there...no matter how busy it was. And if it weren't busy, Jen would still be busy cleaning and organizing things. Her favorite thing to say was, *we work as a team.* These words would serve us well over the years.

At one point, I transferred to the Operating Room (OR). Jen wanted to come with me and asked me to put in a good word for her. I went to the Director of the OR and asked him to consider Jen for the position of Surgical Technologist. He was skeptical. The only experience she had was scrubbing for C-sections in Labor and delivery. I told him that Jen would be a perfect fit for the OR. She is hard working and never says no to overtime (I think this is the part that sealed the deal), has an excellent work ethic, is a quick study, and would be an asset to the department. I promised him that he would not be sorry if he hired her.

He took a chance on her, and I was never proven wrong. When the decision was made that Surgical Technologists would have to take a test to be 'certified,' Jen studied like crazy and was the first to get the certification. Similarly, when it was decided that if there was a need to do an emergency hysterectomy during a C-Section, Jen stepped up, learned the procedure, and encouraged her peers to do the same.

My husband and I retired to Florida, and at one point, my mother-in-law needed some help in terms of company and cheer. Jen would routinely check on her and bring her granddaughter with her; a good time was had by all. She would always call and tell me that my mommy was okay, and she would send me pictures of them. It made us feel so good that she was looked after by someone we loved and trusted.

Jen used to love to browse the newspaper for yard sales, where she would find things for almost nothing and give them away to some needy family. Whether you needed a caregiver or a washing machine, Jen did it all! Her garage was full of things that someone might need.

When Jen got sick, we were devastated. I know she suffered terribly but quietly and with grace. She bravely accepted her diagnosis and kept her faith in the Lord.

Love you and miss you, Jen. I'll never forget you and the good times we had.
— *Madeline Henry, RN BSN*

———————◄•

Around 1 am in the operating room on Thanksgiving Day 2018, I was blessed to meet Aunty. We did a surgical case together. She asked me what I was doing for Thanksgiving, and I told her I would be post-call sleeping. I had expressed that I was new to the area and had no family nearby. She immediately exchanged numbers and insisted I come to her family gathering for dinner. That was the beginning of our journey.

She took me in like a daughter and also my younger brother, who was living with me at the time. She called me frequently, checked in on me, prayed for me, sent me fruit, cakes, and patties on random occasions, and ensured I was always doing well.

She was always working; once in a while, she would come to the labor and delivery unit to see me, and everyone would remember when she worked on the unit and how great she was. She was a shining star.

When I met my husband, I was so excited to tell her about him! She told me about her wonderful marriage and stories of how she met her husband and their beautiful journey.

I was so blessed to have known her. She loved our Lord Jesus Christ and was a faithful servant. I miss her dearly but know she is at peace resting in Heaven.

I love you, Aunty. Thank you for all your kindness.
— *Buki Awosika, your Nigerian daughter*

————————◄•

"Who can find a virtuous woman? for her price is far above rubies."– Proverbs 31:10

She was Sister Jennifer Atkinson, but I affectionately called her Sister Jennifer. The very first time I met her was when she came to visit my sick husband in Jamaica, who is now deceased. My life has never been the same.

Sister Jennifer met us with a beautiful smile that changed the entire atmosphere. There was such joy and energy among us. Then and there, I realized she was not an ordinary woman but a true representative of God. I felt she was here on a mission. Not to be served but to serve. And not just in one place but every area she saw a need. This lady's relationship with God was so real and meaningful that it touched other relationships, especially her closest friendships. I thank God for the day he brought her into my life and for the powerful support she had been to me. A life that is well lived brings glory to God here on earth, and that she did. Faithful to the end, she never let go of her faith in God.

To God be the glory!
— *Minister Campbell*

Jennifer was a friend to me. She was always there… whether for advice, help, or just to talk. Her memory will last forever.

— *Icelyn Smith*

Jen…my wonderful friend!! My precious sister in Christ. She called me 'sis.' She gave her time unconditionally to her family and friends. She was everybody's friend, and you would feel special even if you were in the midst of hundreds of her other friends. She had a special place in her heart for each one of us. She gave, shared, taught, and forgave. She was also a counselor when you were faced with difficulties or problems.

I miss her so much, but she left me with many good memories and life lessons: be kind, don't judge, help when you can, give always, and share. I'm so grateful to have known her.

Till we meet again, sis.

— *Sister Olga*

————————◄•

When I think of Sister Jennifer Atkinson, the word LOVE comes immediately to my mind, and this verse, John 13:35 NLT. It says *"Your love for one another will prove to the world that you are my disciples."* She inspired me by helping others and serving her community and people internationally. Sister Jennifer went far beyond the call of duty to support, love, and help others. She used her professional healthcare skills to help people as well! She did this with respect and compassion, which expressed the love of GOD in her.

Even though she may have been experiencing pain, Sister Jennifer always had time to talk to me, encourage me in my ministry, and we would pray for each other and our families! She will be remembered for her incredible smile and beautiful, kind heart.

In loving memories of you, my dear friend (John 15:12).
— *Pastor Maeola*

————————◄•

Jennifer was a woman with a servant's heart—full of love. She cared about others and blessed them even when she had no time. She managed to fit into her schedule whatever was needed to help others.

I remember her telling me, "Anne, you work hard and need a good lunch." One day, she came to my office with a hot meal: Jamaican Jerk Chicken and Ginger Soda. Her food was delicious, though what touched my heart was her caring for me and doing all this for me before going to work. She had to work every day and, at times, a lot of hours standing on her feet in the operating room.

Loving people and making them feel special is what Jennifer did best.

— *Sister Anne Carjigas*

————————◄•

I remember so many wonderful things about Jennifer, aka 'Mommy,' but this one stood out. She had a heart for people. Her love for mankind was larger than life! I got married and moved to Florida with my daughter, and after a year, the marriage ended, and I was thrown on the streets with my daughter! So, I sought help from my local church, which I got while I contemplated my next course of action. So I wrote Jennifer because I trusted her and let her know my situation. She encouraged me to come back to New York, and she would help me get settled. I was embarrassed and didn't want to be a burden, so I declined the invitation. She took up a love offering for me and mailed it. I was so touched and blessed simultaneously. I did not expect that. It enabled me to provide for myself and my daughter until I figured things out.

That act of kindness has resonated with me over the years, and I smile often when I think of her. I strive to be like her by letting others see Christ in me.

Rest in peace, sweet Mommy.
— *Mrs. Joan Ann Marie Miller Green*

My testimony of Aunt Jennifer was from childhood. She was always a radiant, beautiful, loving, compassionate woman of God. She was generous, caring, and thoughtful of everyone around her. Her family, her coworkers, neighbors, friends, and anyone she came in contact with, she left them with a lasting impression of her genuine kindness. She was a wonderful role model of a Proverbs woman...a wife, mother, grandmother, and friend to many.

Her missionary work was impactful, as she worked in the medical and health field. When machinery, or medical equipment and supplies weren't needed any longer at the hospital, she shipped them to third world countries, where poverty is unprecedented. She was always thinking of ways to bless the less unfortunate, and forgotten.

She was a hard worker and spent many hours working overtime at the hospital. Each time I had a baby, she showed up in the operating room to give support and to make sure I was receiving the best care before, during, and after childbirth. She was very well respected by physicians, surgeons, and all medical staff. Everyone knew and loved Aunt Jennifer for her work ethic and sweet spirit.

I honored her several years ago at a Leaders and Legends award event at the Poughkeepsie High School. She was among 35 people honored. Her category was for her humanitarian work overseas and her service, occupation, and ministry in the health field.

It broke our hearts to learn that Aunt Jennifer had become sick. She fiercely fought the illness, and stood on her relentless faith in God. When she was called home to be with the Lord, we were deeply saddened and her absence was deeply felt by all that knew and loved her.

She was a true gift, and her life is a testament and inspiration of what LOVE looks like in action. I will always reflect and follow her example of servitude and love for all. That was her passion and legacy.

— *Ondie James*
————————————◄•

Mrs. Jennifer, I would say, was a lady of standards and well respected. She was like a mother to me. Someone I could count on for advice. She didn't give up on me when the world turned its back on me. She showed me that in this life and world we live in today, it's only because of Jesus that there's life and hope in any situation and that family means everything.

— *Delroy aka Steven*
————————————◄•

"...As for me and my house, we will serve the Lord."
– Joshua 24:15

"For God so loved the world that He gave His only begotten Son, that whoever believes in Him should not perish but have everlasting life." – John 3:16

"That if you confess with your mouth the Lord Jesus and believe in your heart that God has raised Him from the dead, you will be saved. For with the heart one believes unto righteousness, and with the mouth confession is made unto salvation."– Romans 10:9-10

I am an herbalist who promotes natural health and wellness the way God intended. I give the glory to God in all that I do and seek His Kingdom first.

I had come to know Jennifer, her husband Keith, and their amazing daughter Colette. We first spoke on the phone, and I immediately knew this was a God-appointed encounter. When I first met them, the Holy Spirit led me to ask if we could pray, and pray we all did. I was amazed at the peace Jennifer had. It could only be explained as she had the Peace of Christ that surpassed all understanding.

Jennifer was a Godly woman, a brave woman, a woman who was incredibly Spirit-filled and Spirit-led. She was a presence that could not be explained by words or by the flesh but was seen as a presence with an anointing from God. She was truly an inspiration not only in how to live but also an example of confidence, knowing where she was going when she would die, with certainty knowing that she would be going home to be with the Lord.

It was not until I had attended Jennifer's funeral that I learned how God had used her to do so much for so many with so little, but with God, all things are possible. Everyone in attendance, including close friends and family, was shocked by the presented testimonies. It literally put tears in my eyes to hear of the multitudes that she had helped. All Glory be to God!

My friendship and fellowship with my Sister in Christ, Colette, has continued out of this God encounter. I have watched her turn this trial into a testimony and witnessed her love for the Lord move her with a powerful anointing and her desire to do so much for His kingdom.

God bless you, Colette, and your entire family. I look forward to seeing all of the great things that Christ will help you accomplish.

And since I started off this testimony with the living word of God in scripture, let me leave you with this as I believe it explains all of Jennifer's actions that she had done with a cheerful heart.

"Do not lay up for yourselves treasures on earth, where moth

and rust destroy and where thieves break in and steal; but lay up for yourselves treasures in heaven, where neither moth nor rust destroys and where thieves do not break in and steal"
– Matthew 6:19-20

Jennifer: "Well done, good, and faithful servant…"

Humbly in His service,
— *Ron Buffone*
———————◄•

Jennifer was one of my customers at ShopRite. I want to pay tribute to a kind soul, an indulgent heart, and a disciplined mind. Thank you for coming into my life and loving me. Thank you for all the memories. I will never forget them, but I will cherish them forever. I do not want to dwell on the sorrow of her departure but celebrate her life, love, and spirit. I will remember her as a friend, an inspiration, and a guiding light. She was a force of nature that changed the world around her. She was a woman who believed in the power of love and kindness and who lived her life inspiring others to believe the same. Let's remember her for who she truly was: an extraordinary woman, an inspiring friend, and a beacon of light that will continue to shine brightly in our hearts.

— *Selina*
———————◄•

REFLECTIONS OF THE LIFE OF JENNIFER ATKINSON

On June 30, 1957, Jennifer Ivoree Young Atkinson, also known as "Moy," was born to Hyacinth Wiggan and Rupert Young in Westmoreland, Jamaica, West Indies. She attended Savanna-La-Mar Primary School and then Savanna-La-Mar Secondary, which is now Godfrey Stewart High School. Even as a teenager, Jennifer was recognized for her dedicated academic accomplishment and was nominated by her teachers as an outstanding student in which she nominated to be a "perfect" the last two years of high school. After graduating, she attended St. James Commercial Institute in Montego Bay.

In 1976, she migrated to Canada, where she met her dearly beloved husband, Keith Atkinson. They were married on August 7th, 1976, and then later moved to the United States of America. In 1984, she became a citizen and decided to make New York her home state. Jennifer has always loved and desired God. In 1996, Jennifer accepted Jesus Christ as her Lord and Savior and was baptized at the Faith Assembly of God in Poughkeepsie, New York. She remained an active member at Faith Assembly to the end. She was passionate about medical missions and was involved in the Rotary

Club, where she assisted in sending medical supplies to hospitals throughout Jamaica and many other third-world countries.

Jennifer was a dedicated worker at Vassar Brothers Medical Center in Poughkeepsie, NY for over thirty-nine years. During that time, she obtained her Associate Degree in Arts and Science. She loved her job, but most importantly, she loved her coworkers even more. She was passionate about her cooking and always making sure everyone was fed. She adapted everyone as family. Her favorite holiday was Thanksgiving. This was the time she would cook and celebrate with her friends and family. Not only did Jennifer love cooking, but she also loved to travel with her family and friends annually to "The Cruisers," shopping and watching HGTV. She always sought new ideas to decorate her home and help others do the same. She had a heart of gold, always giving and helping others in any area she could.

It was in the spring of 2019 that Jennifer's health began to decline. She was diagnosed with pancreatic cancer. Although the news was devasting and the journey ahead was rough, she never lost her faith, trust, and love for Christ. The anchor in her soul stood firm in Christ Jesus.

The battle with cancer was over on January 22, 2020, when God gently called her Home. She left behind her loving husband, Keith; Daughters, Kristina and Colette; Grandchildren, Demoya and Daniel; Son-in-law, Andrew Smith. Sisters: Paulette & Sharon Green, Sandra, Annie, Maxine, Sereta, Jem Young, Sandra Davidson, Carol Reddicks Brothers: Glen Ford Snow, Paul Green, Paul, Leroy, Joey, Ranny, David, Weston, Tony and Dan Young with aunties, uncles, neices, nephews, cousins many other relatives, and a host of friends. As a matter of information it is noteworthy that her mother, Hyacinth Wiggan had 5 children and Father, Rupert Young had 27 children. Jennifer's mother passed away on May 7, 2021 and Father passed away on September 13, 1996.

JENNIFER IVOREE ATKINSON
June 30, 1957 - January 22, 2020

Bibliography

1. Schizas, D., Charalampakis, N., Kole, C., Economopoulou, P., Koustas, E., Gkotsis, E., Ziogas, D., Psyrri, A., & Karamouzis, M. V. (2020, April 2). Immunotherapy for pancreatic cancer: A 2020 update, Cancer Treatment Reviews, Volume 86, 2020, 102016, ISSN 0305-7372, https://doi. Org/10.1016/j.Ctrv.2020.102016. ScienceDirect. Retrieved December 2, 2024, from https://www.sciencedirect.com/science/article/pii/S0305737220300542

www.ingramcontent.com/pod-product-compliance
Lightning Source LLC
Chambersburg PA
CBHW052120090426
42741CB00009B/1886